SHIPS

Written by Richard Humble
Illustrated by Peter Cornwall

RSVP

**RAINTREE
STECK-VAUGHN**
P U B L I S H E R S
The Steck-Vaughn Company

Austin, Texas

Editor: Frank Tarsitano
Project Manager: Julie Klaus

Library of Congress Cataloging-in-Publication Data
Humble, Richard.
      Ships / written by Richard Humble; illustrated by Peter Cornwall.
         p.   cm. — (Pointers)
      Includes index.
      Summary: Analyzes the structure of and provides historical information for a wide variety of vessels, from ancient Egyptian warships and Greek triremes to modern aircraft carriers and ocean liners.
    ISBN 0-8114-6158-0
    1. Ships — Juvenile literature.   2. Ships — History — Juvenile literature. [1. Ships.]   I. Cornwall, Peter, ill. II. Title.
VM150.H86   1994
387.2—dc20   93-19705
                                    CIP

Printed and bound in the United States

1 2 3 4 5 6 7 8 9 0 VH 99 98 97 96 95 94 93

Foreword

This book tells the story of the oldest form of long-distance transportation – the ship. Since the time of the ancient Egyptians, ships have been carrying people and their goods across the oceans of the world. For most of the 5,000 years since then, men have also built ships of war, designed to win control of the sea in naval battles.

The first ships were simple craft, driven by a single sail and light enough to be rowed as well as sailed. By the late 15th century, bigger ships with more than one mast and roomy cargo holds were able to cross the world's oceans. Ships of that time were also being armed with the latest weapon of land warfare – the cannon. For the next 350 years, sea battles were fought between fleets of wooden sailing ships armed with two or three decks of heavy guns.

About 150 years ago, the ship was transformed. Steam power and the new technology of building with iron and steel arrived. The new steamships soon brought the age of sail to an end. The story continues into the 20th century with the aircraft carrier, the submarine, and the most luxurious form of travel ever known – the passenger liner.

Contents

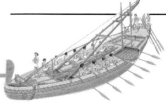

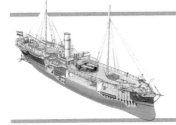

Egyptian Warships

Below is one of the ships that was sent to attack Syria by Sahure, pharaoh of Egypt, in about 2400 B.C. The ancient Egyptians were great sailors and left many pictures showing how they built boats and ships nearly 5,000 years ago.

They were the first people to build open wooden ships with a big square sail to catch the wind and oars for rowing in harbors and calm weather. Although it was improved greatly over the centuries, the same sort of ship was still being used by the Vikings 3,500 years later.

3 The high bow post of Egypt's warships carried the "all-seeing eye" — a good-luck charm believed to bring the ship safely home.

2 A belt of twisted rope was stretched tightly around the hull above the waterline. This helped to keep the planks firmly together. It gave the hull more strength.

1 The narrow bow is a weak point because it takes the full force of the waves. The Egyptians made their boats stronger by tying a tightly twisted rope under the bow from side to side.

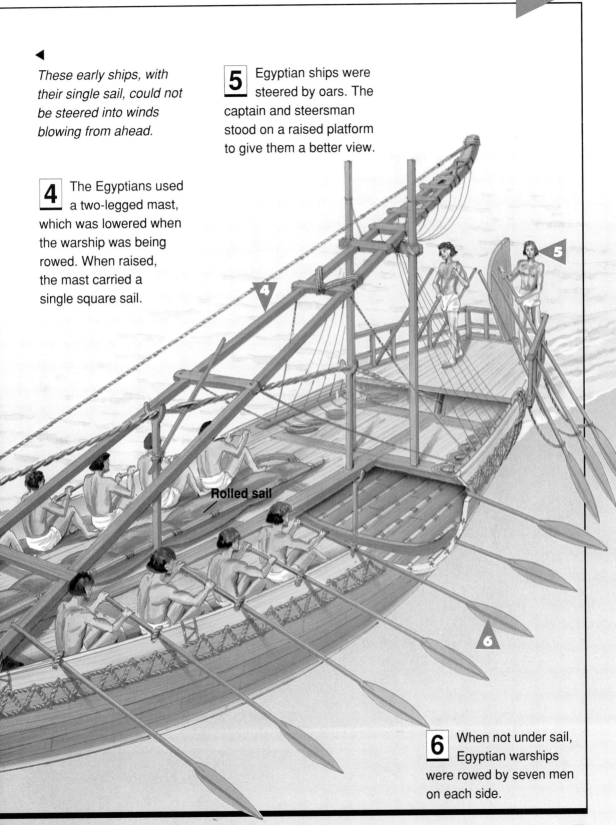

These early ships, with their single sail, could not be steered into winds blowing from ahead.

5 Egyptian ships were steered by oars. The captain and steersman stood on a raised platform to give them a better view.

4 The Egyptians used a two-legged mast, which was lowered when the warship was being rowed. When raised, the mast carried a single square sail.

Rolled sail

6 When not under sail, Egyptian warships were rowed by seven men on each side.

Greek Triremes

By 500 B.C., the Greeks had become the first seafaring people to build a ship designed specially for fighting at sea. This was the trireme, a light, fast war galley which had a pointed ram jutting from its bow. The ship was called a trireme because it had three rows, or banks, of oars. The trireme was used to smash and sink enemy ships in battle.

In 480 B.C. the Greek trireme fleet saved Greece from conquest by the Persian Empire. It destroyed a powerful Persian fleet in a famous sea battle at Salamis.

▶

The trireme had a special device called an outrigger stretching out from the ship's side. This enabled such a narrow ship to carry so many oars in more than one bank.

2 The ship was usually steered by twin stern oars. To make a sharp turn, the rowers on one side would stop while those on the other side continued rowing.

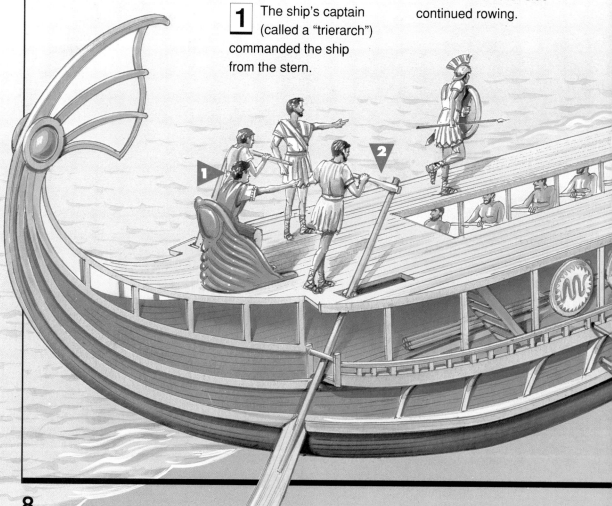

1 The ship's captain (called a "trierarch") commanded the ship from the stern.

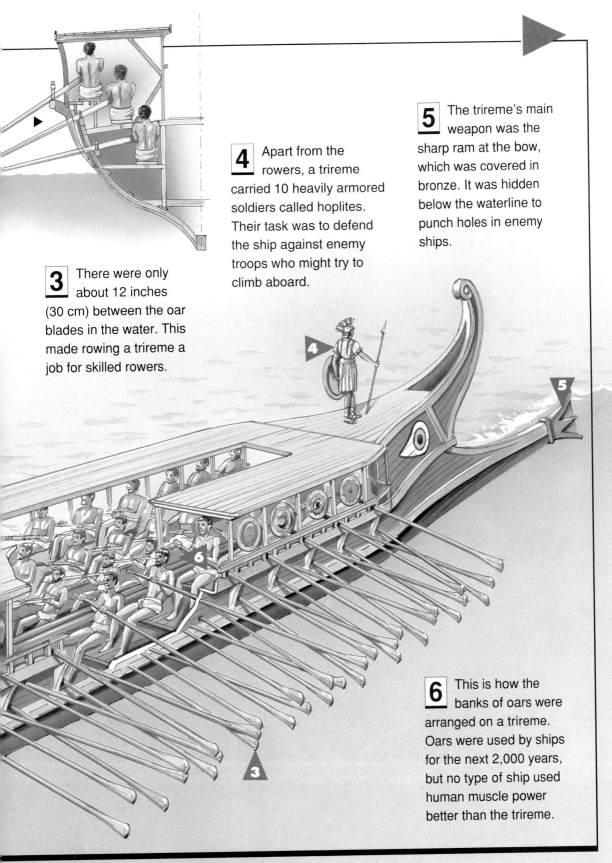

4 Apart from the rowers, a trireme carried 10 heavily armored soldiers called hoplites. Their task was to defend the ship against enemy troops who might try to climb aboard.

5 The trireme's main weapon was the sharp ram at the bow, which was covered in bronze. It was hidden below the waterline to punch holes in enemy ships.

3 There were only about 12 inches (30 cm) between the oar blades in the water. This made rowing a trireme a job for skilled rowers.

6 This is how the banks of oars were arranged on a trireme. Oars were used by ships for the next 2,000 years, but no type of ship used human muscle power better than the trireme.

Viking Long Ships

The Viking long ship was built in Denmark, Norway, and Sweden from about 700 A.D. to 1000 A.D. It was an open ship with a single mast and sail. The hull was made from overlapping planks. Hulls built in this way are called "clinker-built."

The long ship was either sailed or rowed (both are shown here). Viking explorers crossed the Atlantic Ocean in this type of ship and reached Iceland, Greenland, and North America (which the Vikings called "Vinland"). The ship could also be rowed up river. Long ships were even dragged overland to reach Russia's great rivers.

3 Vikings often decorated their ships with rich and beautiful carvings.

2 The hull of the overlapping planks was built to withstand the pounding of heavy seas in the Atlantic Ocean.

1 When the sail and mast had been lowered, the long ship was rowed using about 15 pairs of oars.

Chests used as rowing benches

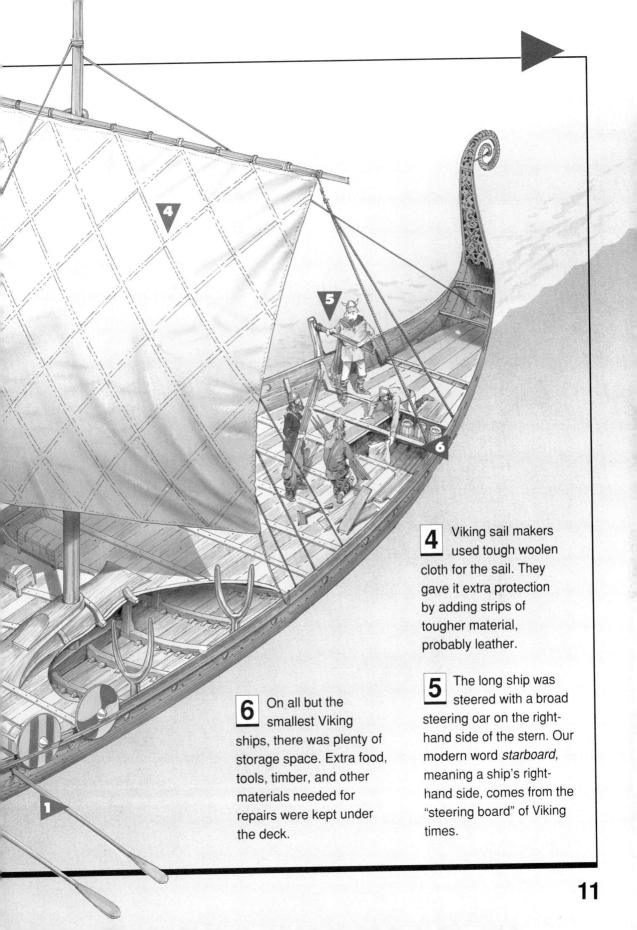

4 Viking sail makers used tough woolen cloth for the sail. They gave it extra protection by adding strips of tougher material, probably leather.

5 The long ship was steered with a broad steering oar on the right-hand side of the stern. Our modern word *starboard*, meaning a ship's right-hand side, comes from the "steering board" of Viking times.

6 On all but the smallest Viking ships, there was plenty of storage space. Extra food, tools, timber, and other materials needed for repairs were kept under the deck.

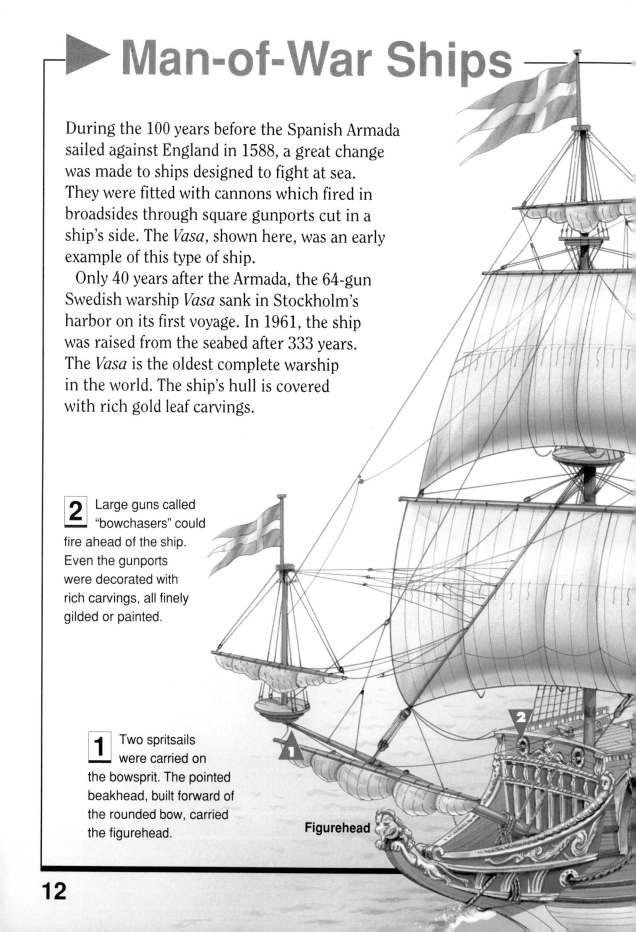

Man-of-War Ships

During the 100 years before the Spanish Armada sailed against England in 1588, a great change was made to ships designed to fight at sea. They were fitted with cannons which fired in broadsides through square gunports cut in a ship's side. The *Vasa*, shown here, was an early example of this type of ship.

Only 40 years after the Armada, the 64-gun Swedish warship *Vasa* sank in Stockholm's harbor on its first voyage. In 1961, the ship was raised from the seabed after 333 years. The *Vasa* is the oldest complete warship in the world. The ship's hull is covered with rich gold leaf carvings.

2 Large guns called "bowchasers" could fire ahead of the ship. Even the gunports were decorated with rich carvings, all finely gilded or painted.

1 Two spritsails were carried on the bowsprit. The pointed beakhead, built forward of the rounded bow, carried the figurehead.

Figurehead

3 The crew lived and ate their meals beside their guns on the lower gun decks. They slept in hammocks slung from the deck beams above.

4 The *Vasa* carried a triangular "lateen" sail on her mizzenmast. European ship designers had copied this type of sail from the Arabs, whose sailing dhows still use it today.

5 When the *Vasa* was raised from the seabed in 1961, thousands of items belonging to the crew were found inside. The bones of 18 people trapped below deck when the *Vasa* sank were also found.

6 The lower row of gunports in the *Vasa's* slim hull were too close to the water. When the ship tilted too far to one side, water flooded in and sank the *Vasa*.

Rudder

Anchor

Ships of the Line

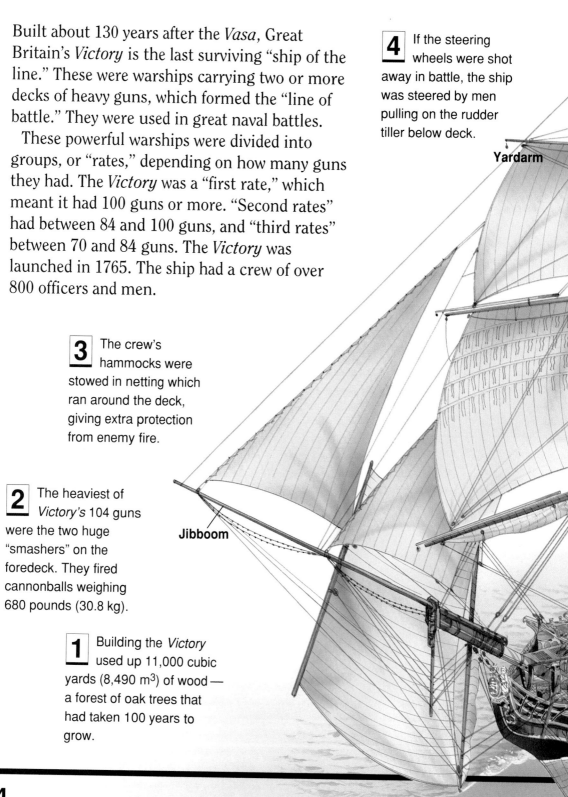

Built about 130 years after the *Vasa*, Great Britain's *Victory* is the last surviving "ship of the line." These were warships carrying two or more decks of heavy guns, which formed the "line of battle." They were used in great naval battles.

These powerful warships were divided into groups, or "rates," depending on how many guns they had. The *Victory* was a "first rate," which meant it had 100 guns or more. "Second rates" had between 84 and 100 guns, and "third rates" between 70 and 84 guns. The *Victory* was launched in 1765. The ship had a crew of over 800 officers and men.

4 If the steering wheels were shot away in battle, the ship was steered by men pulling on the rudder tiller below deck.

Yardarm

3 The crew's hammocks were stowed in netting which ran around the deck, giving extra protection from enemy fire.

2 The heaviest of *Victory's* 104 guns were the two huge "smashers" on the foredeck. They fired cannonballs weighing 680 pounds (30.8 kg).

Jibboom

1 Building the *Victory* used up 11,000 cubic yards (8,490 m³) of wood — a forest of oak trees that had taken 100 years to grow.

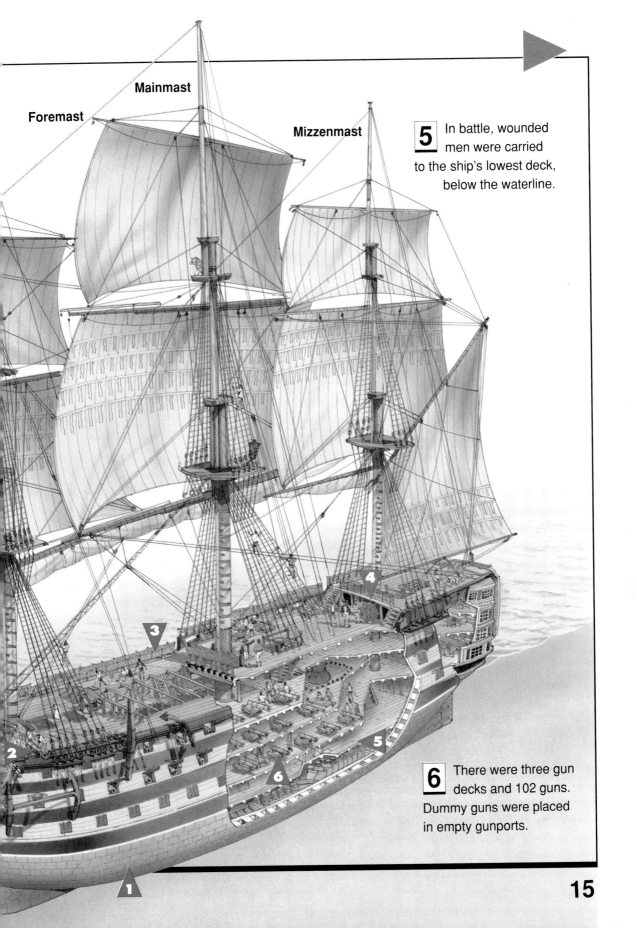

Foremast

Mainmast

Mizzenmast

5 In battle, wounded men were carried to the ship's lowest deck, below the waterline.

6 There were three gun decks and 102 guns. Dummy guns were placed in empty gunports.

15

Early Steamships

Few other ships have ever achieved so many "firsts" as the *Great Britain*, built in 1843. It was the first large ship (about 4,000 tons) to be build entirely of iron; the first to be driven by a propeller instead of by side paddle wheels; the first to use watertight compartments as a safety measure; and the first to be given bilge keels.

The *Great Britain* made its first Atlantic crossing in 1845 and was in use for nearly 40 years. It carried both passengers and cargo on its voyages.

1 The *Great Britain's* screw propeller was very advanced for its time. Instead of the simple two-bladed screw carried by most steamships, The *Great Britain's* was six-bladed.

Lifeboat

Engine

2 The *Great Britain* was also the first modern passenger liner. It had staterooms (luxury cabins) for 60 passengers who traveled in first-class comfort.

3 Like all other early steamships, the *Great Britain* did not rely solely on engines for power. The ship could also carry almost 15,000 square feet (1,393 sq m) of sail on six masts.

4 To improve its performance in high seas, the *Great Britain* had a very sharp bow.

5 Bilge keels made the ship roll less in rough weather and made sailing more comfortable.

6 The ships roomy hull was divided into six compartments by watertight bulkheads as a safety precaution.

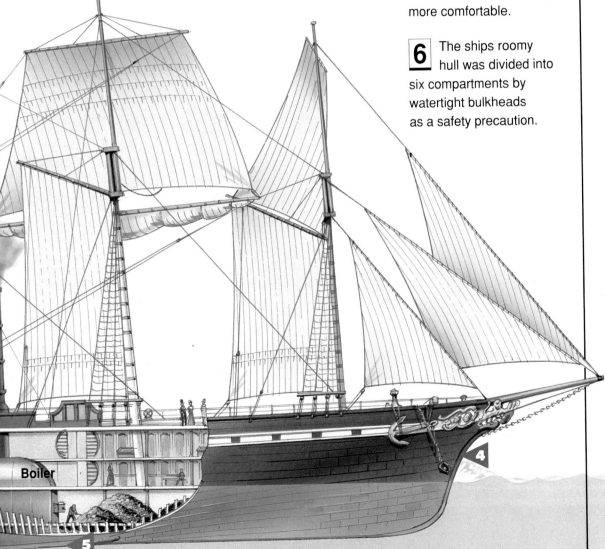

Boiler

Clipper Ships

"Clippers" were so called because they were the fastest sailing ships in the world and were able to "clip" days off the sailing time of any other ship. They were built to transport passengers and cargo over long distances in the shortest possible time.

Clippers carried Americans to California around Cape Horn, Australian wool to Great Britain, and tea from China to London. The record London-to-Australia voyage was 60 days. Clippers were widely used between 1850 and 1870. However, they could not travel as fast or carry as much cargo as the new steamships.

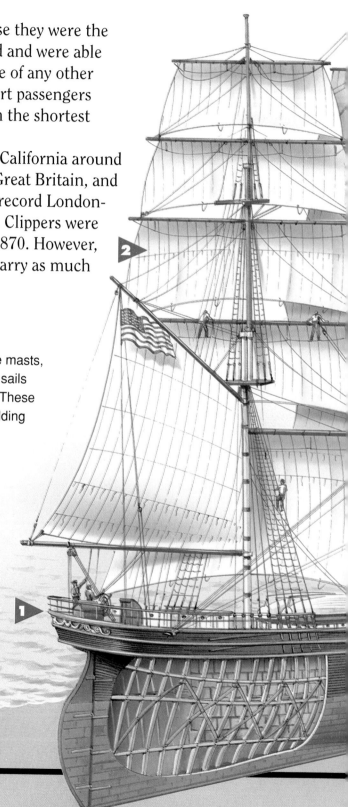

3 On all three masts, small extra sails could be added. These were called "studding sails."

2 Named from the bottom upward, the basic sails on the mainmast were the mainsail, the topsail, the gallant, and the royal.

1 Built to provide extra strength, the ship's overhanging counterstern helped protect this part of the ship from waves.

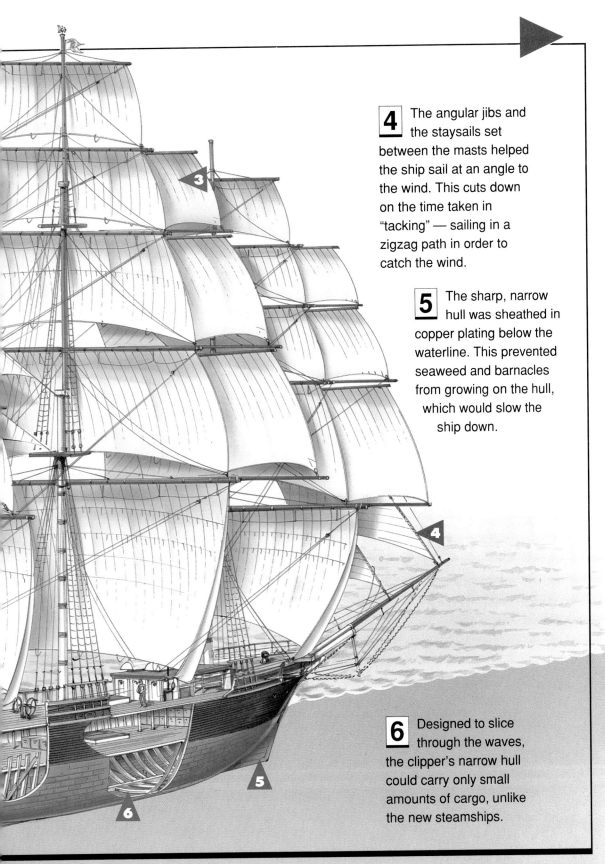

4 The angular jibs and the staysails set between the masts helped the ship sail at an angle to the wind. This cuts down on the time taken in "tacking" — sailing in a zigzag path in order to catch the wind.

5 The sharp, narrow hull was sheathed in copper plating below the waterline. This prevented seaweed and barnacles from growing on the hull, which would slow the ship down.

6 Designed to slice through the waves, the clipper's narrow hull could carry only small amounts of cargo, unlike the new steamships.

Ironclads

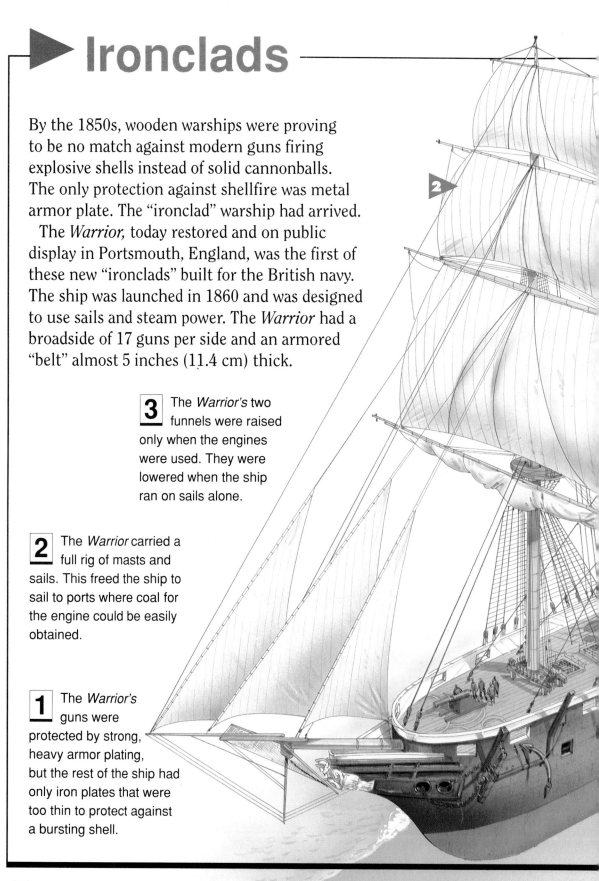

By the 1850s, wooden warships were proving to be no match against modern guns firing explosive shells instead of solid cannonballs. The only protection against shellfire was metal armor plate. The "ironclad" warship had arrived.

The *Warrior,* today restored and on public display in Portsmouth, England, was the first of these new "ironclads" built for the British navy. The ship was launched in 1860 and was designed to use sails and steam power. The *Warrior* had a broadside of 17 guns per side and an armored "belt" almost 5 inches (11.4 cm) thick.

3 The *Warrior's* two funnels were raised only when the engines were used. They were lowered when the ship ran on sails alone.

2 The *Warrior* carried a full rig of masts and sails. This freed the ship to sail to ports where coal for the engine could be easily obtained.

1 The *Warrior's* guns were protected by strong, heavy armor plating, but the rest of the ship had only iron plates that were too thin to protect against a bursting shell.

4 A hollow space at the stern enabled the ship's propeller to be disconnected and hoisted for long voyages under sail only. This prevented the propeller from slowing the ship like a brake when not being used.

Ventilator

5 The armored belt was given extra strength on the inside by massive slabs of strong teakwood. These were more than 17 inches (45 cm) thick.

6 The *Warrior's* engines used so much coal that the ship's storage bunkers were designed to carry 935 tons of it. The *Warrior's* best speed was just over 14 knots (16 mph).

Turret Rams

Launched in 1868, only seven years after the *Warrior,* the ironclad ship *Buffel* (the name means buffalo) was built in Great Britain for the Dutch navy. The *Buffel* was one of the world's first warships to be driven by steam only. The ship also carried two heavy guns in a rotating turret.

For nearly 300 years, warships had fought with their guns rather than by ramming enemy ships, as ancient oared galleys had done. By the 1860s, however, steam-engined ships with steel hulls made ramming attacks possible again, and the *Buffel* had a strengthened bow for ramming. But the ship never saw battle, and today it is a museum ship in Rotterdam in the Netherlands.

3 The two sailors manning the ship's steering wheel at the back of the ship were completely exposed to the weather and enemy fire. Steering the ship would have been very uncomfortable in bad weather.

2 The *Buffel* was one of the first warships in the world to be driven by twin propellers. Each propeller was driven by a separate engine. The ship could travel at over 12 knots (14 mph) in a calm sea. This was extremely fast for the late 1860s.

1 Below decks there was plenty of living space for the crew and separate cabins for the officers. The *Buffel* was later used as a floating barracks for Dutch navy sailors.

4 The *Buffel* was commanded from a light, open bridge running from side to side across the center of the ship. This provided an excellent all-around view but gave no protection against bad weather or enemy fire.

5 The circular turret contained two heavy guns firing shells 9 inches (23 cm) wide. The turret could turn from side to side to fire on the enemy.

6 The *Buffel's* main weapon, after its guns, was the armored ram bow, jutting forward below the waterline. It was designed both to withstand the force of enemy shells and to survive the tremendous shock of a ramming attack.

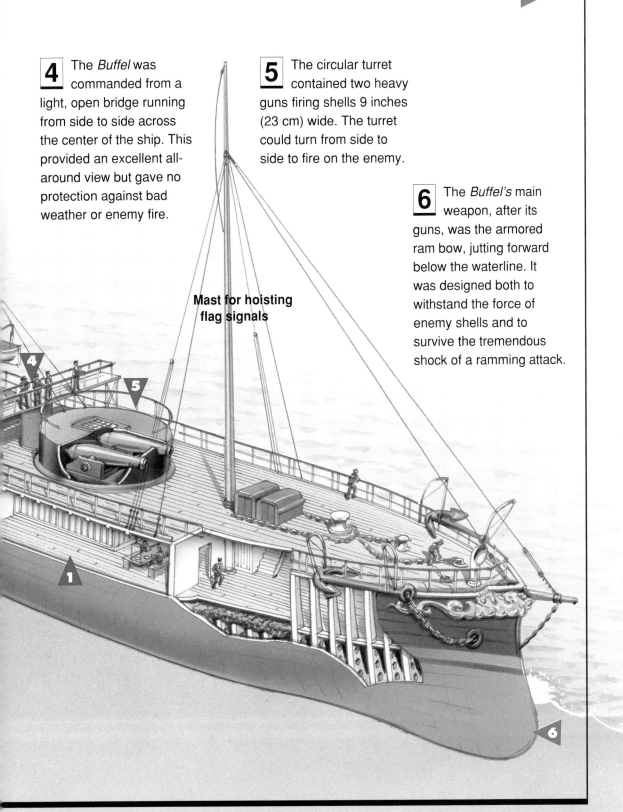

Mast for hoisting flag signals

Submarines

The submarine shown here is a Type VII German U-boat, or *Unterseebooten*, from World War II (1939–1945). Like all submarines, the U-boat dived by flooding tanks on the side of the hull with seawater and surfaced by blowing the tanks with compressed air. Submarines carried torpedoes, which were fired against enemy ships. The fired, torpedoes ran below the water's surface and burst against the hull of the target ship.

The first successful submarines used gasoline engines on the surface and electric motors running on batteries when submerged. Later submarines used diesel engines, which were more powerful.

2 When on the ocean surface, powerful diesel engines drove the U-boat at 16 knots (18.5 mph).

3 When lying just below the surface, the U-boat captain raised the periscope to look for targets. The periscope was lowered when the U-boat dived.

Gun for surface fighting

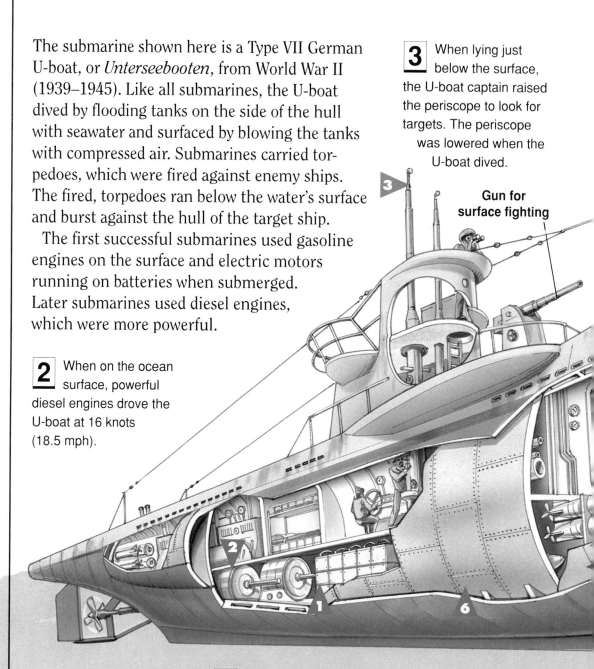

1 The batteries for the electric motors were recharged by the diesel engines each time the U-boat surfaced.

6 The ballast tanks, which took in water when the U-boat dived, surrounded the inner hull where the crew lived.

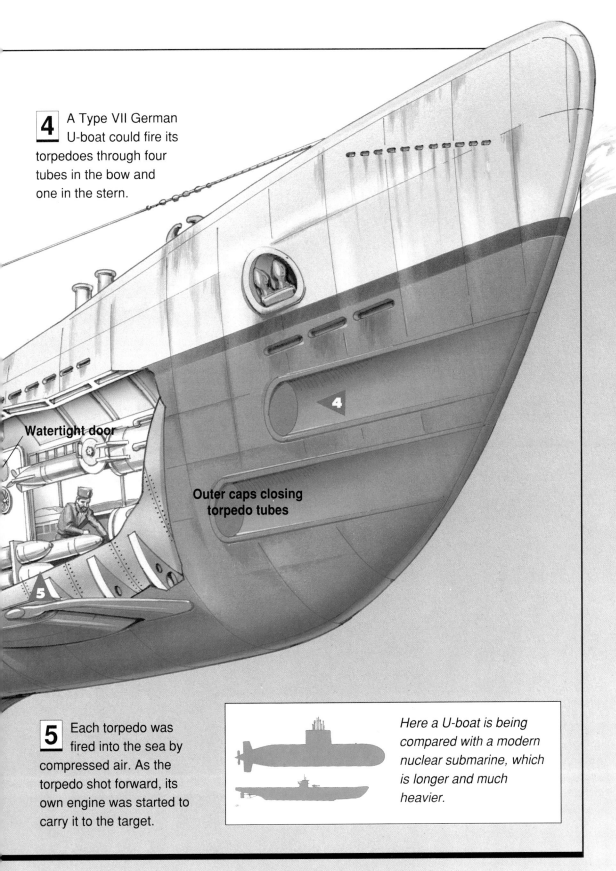

4 A Type VII German U-boat could fire its torpedoes through four tubes in the bow and one in the stern.

Watertight door

Outer caps closing torpedo tubes

5 Each torpedo was fired into the sea by compressed air. As the torpedo shot forward, its own engine was started to carry it to the target.

Here a U-boat is being compared with a modern nuclear submarine, which is longer and much heavier.

Aircraft Carriers

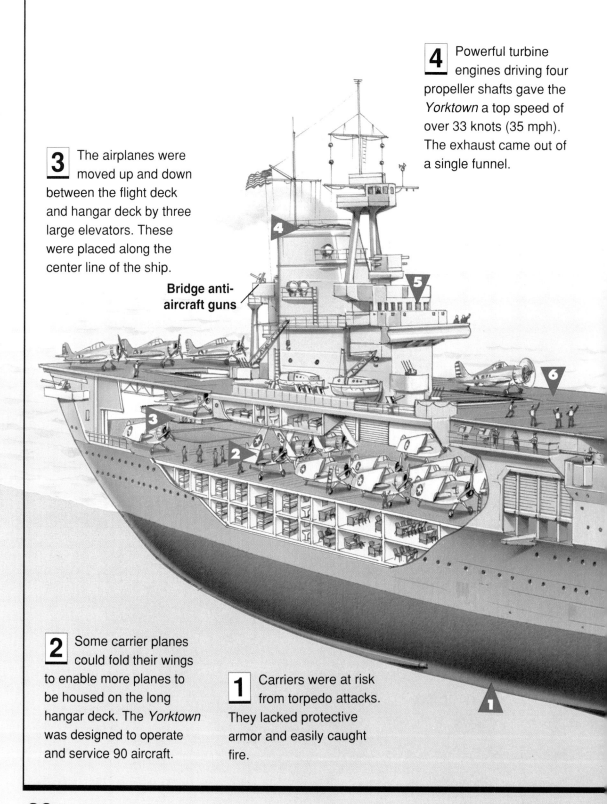

4 Powerful turbine engines driving four propeller shafts gave the *Yorktown* a top speed of over 33 knots (35 mph). The exhaust came out of a single funnel.

3 The airplanes were moved up and down between the flight deck and hangar deck by three large elevators. These were placed along the center line of the ship.

Bridge anti-aircraft guns

2 Some carrier planes could fold their wings to enable more planes to be housed on the long hangar deck. The *Yorktown* was designed to operate and service 90 aircraft.

1 Carriers were at risk from torpedo attacks. They lacked protective armor and easily caught fire.

5 Called the "island," the carrier's bridge and funnel structure was placed on the starboard side of the ship.

6 To launch and recover airplanes, the carrier had to steam at full speed into the wind. Catapults, powered by compressed steam, were used to launch some airplanes.

The aircraft carrier was developed during the final years of World War I (1914–1918). It gave fleets the power to launch air attacks on enemy ships, while defending themselves from enemy air attack. In World War II (1939–1945) rival fleets with aircraft carriers fought major battles without the ships of either fleet ever sighting each other.

An aircraft carrier is a floating air base. It has large stocks of aircraft fuel and weapons, a hangar deck to which aircraft can be lowered for repairs, and an upper flight deck, where the aircraft take off and land. Shown here is the famous American carrier *Yorktown,* completed in 1937.

Bow anti-aircraft guns

Ocean Liners

Developed in the late 1800s, the passenger liner became a major means of travel. The most frequently used travel route was across the Atlantic between the United States and Europe. The world's greatest liners competed for the "Blue Ribbon of the Atlantic," awarded for the fastest crossing.

Because airplanes can travel so fast, ocean liners have become less important for travel. But ocean liners, or cruise ships, are popular for luxury vacations at sea.

3 Since the luxury liner *Titanic* sank with the loss of over 1,500 lives in 1912, the law requires all passenger liners to carry enough lifeboats and emergency rafts to hold all passengers and crew members.

Sundeck

Swimming pools

Theater

Discotheque

2 Rough weather causes the ship to pitch from bow to stern, and roll from side to side. Modern cruise liners are fitted with winglike stabilizers to help reduce these movements.

1 The engines are designed to be very quiet, smooth, and economical. Luxury liners no longer need high-speed engine power.

4 Modern ships have better aids for safe navigation than at any time in history. These include radar and electronic navigation systems using special orbiting satellites out in space.

5 A modern cruise ship is designed to give passengers every possible enjoyment. It has restaurants, lounges, playrooms for children, movies, indoor and outdoor sports, and at least one swimming pool.

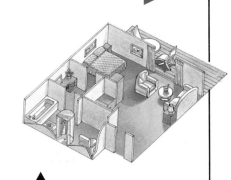

▲

A deluxe cabin offers passengers the facilities of any luxury hotel suite to be found ashore.

6 The sharp "clipper bow" parts high waves rather than crashing into them. Below the surface, the ship has a rounded, bulbous bow. This also helps the ship to remain stable.

Glossary

Ballast tanks
Tanks which are flooded to make a submarine dive, and are pumped full of air to make it surface

Beakhead
Pointed structure built out from a sailing ship's bow

Bilge keels
Long narrow plates on the underside of a ship, on either side of the central keel

Bow
The pointed front end of a ship

Bow post
The strong timber rising from the front of a wooden ship's keel

Bowchaser
A gun placed to fire straight ahead of the ship

Bowsprit
Large spar mounted in a sailing ship's bow, from which spritsails or jibs are set (attached)

Bridge
Raised platform on the deck of a ship, from which the ship is commanded

Broadside
All the guns on one side of a ship, arranged to fire together

Bulkhead
A wall between compartments and cabins inside a ship

Counterstern
A ship's stern which is high and curved, instead of square

Deck beam
The beams running from side to side in a ship, supporting the decks

Dhow
A type of Arab sailing ship with lateen sails

Figurehead
Ornamental carved figure, mounted on the beakhead of a sailing ship

Foredeck
The forward deck of a ship, often raised above the level of the upper deck

Gallants
The sails set above the topsails

Galley
A ship's kitchen; also a light, narrow warship driven by oars

Gunport
A square hole cut in a ship's side for a gun to fire through

Head wind
A wind blowing onto the bow of a ship, making progress difficult

Hull
The main body of a ship, supporting masts and rigging

Island
The bridge structure of an aircraft carrier, placed to the side of the flight deck

Jibs
Small triangular sails, set between a ship's foremast and bowsprit

Kites
Small extra sails set to get the most speed from the wind in good weather

Lateen sail
A large triangular sail, running fore and aft, carried on a long slanting yard

Line of battle
The line formed by a fleet's heaviest ships when preparing for battle

Mainsail
The largest square sails of a ship set on the lowest yards

Periscope
A long tube with viewing glasses, for seeing above the surface from a submarine under water

Propeller
The rotating screw which drives an engine-powered ship forward

Ram
A pointed projection for damaging the hull of enemy ships

Royals
The sails set above the gallants

Rudder
The hinged timber or metal plate hung at the stern, for changing the ship's direction

Ship of the line
A sailing battleship with two or more gun decks, powerful enough to join the line of battle

Skysails
The sails set above the royals

Spritsails
The sail or sails set below the bowsprit

Staysails
Triangular sails set between the masts

Stern
A ship's rear end

Studding sails
Small extra sails set on either side of the yards in good weather

Tacking
Steering a zigzag course to make progress against a head wind

Topsails
The sails set above the courses

Torpedo
A missile fired to sink an enemy ship by exploding beneath the waterline

Trireme
A Greek war galley rowed by three levels, banks, or oars

Waterline
A line on a ship's hull marking where the water will reach

Yards
Strong poles hung from the masts, from which the sails are set (attached)

Index